Outdoor Explorers
Shape and Patterns

By Sandy Green   Photography by Chris Fairclough

Contents

W
FRANKLIN WATTS
LONDON • SYDNEY

Sort natural materials

Natural materials are all around us. They each have their own shape, colour and texture.

Gather some natural items such as leaves, pebbles, feathers, twigs and flowers. Sort them by shape: round things, long things and spiky things.

Glossary:
Texture – how something feels.

Think how else you could sort them. What about by colour or by texture? Make rope circles to hold each set of shapes.

Some things fit in two sets. Make the circles overlap to show this. For example, moss is both green and soft. Feathers are both white and long.

I sorted things that were both round and wooden.

3

All about texture

Use your hands to explore natural items.
It is fun to do this without looking.

Get an adult to fill a Hessian sack
with things for you to identify.
Hessian is a natural material.
It feels quite itchy.

Glossary: **Identify** – work
out what something is.

Put your hand in and pick an item. Try to work out what it is. Can you describe its shape and texture?

We identified a feather, a pine cone, a log and a coconut shell.

Woodland mobile

Hang string between two trees to make a woodland mobile.

- Collect sticks and twigs to make a shape to hang on the mobile.

- Tie your sticks together with string.

- What shape will you choose?
- How many sticks would you need to make a square?
- How many for a triangle?
- How could you make a circle?

6

• Use natural materials to decorate your shape. Leaves, feathers, long grass and dandelions all work well.

We made a triangle.

• Hang your shape on a long length of string and watch it twirl in the breeze.

Circles and spirals

Draw circles in the air with your finger. Now draw a spiral.
Circles and spirals are all around you. Can you find some?

What do you see if you drop a pebble into a pond?

Look closely at snail shells. What shape can you see? Trace the shape with your finger.

What shape are dandelions?

Can you find a cut down tree? Each circle across the surface shows a year of the tree's growth. Count the circles to find the tree's age.

Where else can you find circles and spirals?

Look for spider webs

Look for spider webs in bushes and hedges. Some will be tiny, some will be very big.

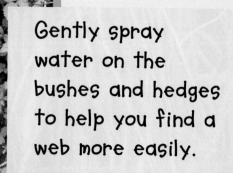

Gently spray water on the bushes and hedges to help you find a web more easily.

Web patterns are always similar. Look closely at a web. Describe its shape and pattern to a friend.

Did you see a spider? Where was it? Often spiders are right in the centre of their web.

Make a spider web

Look carefully at spider webs. How many corners do they have? What shape would you call them?

Make your own spider-web shape using pieces of rope.

You could use twigs instead of rope. These can make good web shapes too. Straight twigs all the same length will work best.

Explore and match leaves

Explore the trees and hedgerows near you. Take a picture chart of leaves with you to help you identify each tree.

- Match the leaves to the chart. Which trees have you found?

- Collect some leaves and look at their shapes.

• Which leaves are the largest? Which leaves are the longest? Which trees do they come from? Count how many points each leaf has.

This oak leaf had the most points.

• Explore the textures of the leaves. Are they rough, spiky, soft, smooth or hairy?

• Make leaf rubbings. Wax crayons are good for this. What else might you use to make a rubbing?

Counting petals

Pick some buttercups from a field where there are lots.

- Glue the petals from a buttercup onto paper and then count them. How many are there?

- Draw a picture of your buttercup with the right number of petals.

- Do all buttercups have the same number of petals? How can you find out?

Find some other flowers and count their petals. How many petals does a daisy have?

Make a natural collage

A natural collage can be made almost anywhere.
You could use the idea to make a special fence.

- Collect natural materials.
  Vines, leaves, twigs and grass
  all work well. Longer items
  are easier to use.

- Collect sticks all the same length. Push them into the ground in a row. Tie sticks across them with string.

- Wrap your natural materials around the sticks. What shapes can you see in your collage? What colours have you used?

How will a collage in autumn be different to a collage in the summer?

This is our collage.

Creating camouflage

Camouflage is looking the same as your surroundings.

Look at these places.
Where could you hide?
What camouflage would
you use?

Can you see me?

- Play hide and seek, but make it harder to find each other by using camouflage.

- Hold twigs and leaves in front of you when hiding behind a tree. Try to become part of the woods. Did anyone see you?

- Put mud on your face. This will help you be camouflaged too. What patterns could you use? How will this help you be camouflaged?

Glossary:
Camouflage – hidden by your nearest surroundings.

How hard was it to find your friends? Could they find you?

Activity ideas

Sort natural materials (pages 2-3)
- Talk about shapes, both two and three dimensional.
- Encourage descriptive language to explain how shapes both look and feel.
- Ask the children to predict what shapes they will find in the garden or outdoor area.
- Help the children develop language for comparison; same as, different to, similar, match, bigger than.

All about texture (pages 4-5)
- Talk to the children about how we normally use all of our senses to give us information. Can they name each of the senses?
- Discuss with the children the importance of not seeing what they are feeling during the 'sack' activity. How difficult do they think it will be?
- Encourage the children to describe what they are feeling before they take it out of the sack.
- Explore other senses in similar ways e.g. who can identify flowers or herbs by smell?

Woodland mobile (pages 6-7)
- Decide together what the word mobile means.
- Talk about shapes and what they would like to make using natural items outside.
- Support younger children in tying their shapes together.
- Talk about similarities and differences between shapes e.g. both squares and rectangles have four straight sides and triangles can have either the same or different length sides.

Circles and spirals (pages 8-9)
- Carefully supervise children near to water if exploring ripples in a pond or stream.
- Count circles in tree trunks together.
- Trace the markings on a snail shell together.
- What flowers have circles or spiral shapes?

Look for spider webs (pages 10-11)
- What can the children tell you about spiders?
- Can they explain how a spider makes its web?
- Explore the garden or outdoor area for spider webs. They will be easier to see after rain, or in the morning when the dew is still on them.
- Provide plant sprays to help them find webs in dense bushes.
- Read stories about spiders. Younger children will enjoy *Emily's Legs* by Dick King-Smith, whereas older children will love *Charlotte's Web* by E.B White.

Make a spider web (pages 12-13)
- Show the children a web, or a picture of a web. How would they describe it? What shape is it? How many corners (or points) does it have?
- Many spiders spin their webs in a spiral. Can the children follow this with their finger?
- Talk about how a spider spins its web. Have the children ever seen this? Can they describe it?
- Provide a range of different items for making webs. Which work best?

Explore and match leaves (pages 14-15)
- Prepare charts of leaves in advance. Ensure they match the trees in your local area.
- Discuss the shape, size and texture of leaves with the children. Encourage descriptive language and introduce new words to them.
- Follow up the leaf rubbings by making rubbings of bark and paths. Encourage the children to compare the rubbings. How are they similar? How do they differ?

Counting petals (pages 16-17)
- Practise counting with younger children. Let them choose how they will count their petals.
- Does each flower type always have the same number of petals? Why do they think this might be?

Make a natural collage (pages 18-19)
- What do the children think they might find to make a natural collage? Where will they find these items?
- Support the children in collecting and erecting the sticks for the collage.
- Talk about the shapes, colours and patterns.
- Talk about the action they are using: weaving, under and over, round and round.
- Photograph the completed collage.
- Make another collage at a different time of year and compare it to the photograph of the previous one. What differences can the children see between them?

Creating camouflage (pages 20-21)
- Who can tell you what camouflage is? Where have they seen camouflage?
- Show them pictures of camouflage in the natural world; chameleons, some snakes, toads.
- Encourage them to think about how they could camouflage themselves in the outdoor area. What ideas do they come up with?
- Ensure children wash well if they have used mud as part of their camouflage.

About this book

Each book in this series provides opportunities to enhance learning and development, supporting the four main principles of the early years foundation stage: a unique child, positive relationships, enabling environments, learning and development.

Children who are given opportunities to try, to explore, to find out about their environment and to learn through both success and error will become resilient, capable, confident and self-assured. The outdoor environment is very much an enabling environment. It provides different approaches to learning in which most children thrive, with many developing greater levels of concentration and engagement in activities than they may demonstrate indoors. The freedom of the outdoors encourages positive relationships in children with both their peers and with adults, and develops independence and inner strength. All six areas of learning and development are supported across the activities in this series. Examples of these can be seen in the charts provided at www.franklinwatts.co.uk.

The activities in this book automatically lend themselves to the introduction of new language, thinking points and questioning. They encourage exploration and investigation, both as an individual, and jointly with others. Many activities can be adapted further to meet specific learning needs.

Further information

Free downloadable activity sheets
Go to www.franklinwatts.co.uk to find these free downloadable activity sheets that accompany the activities:

• An identification chart for some common leaves (pages 14-15).
• A sheet with outlines of flowers that could be used for sticking petals onto (pages 16-17).

Forest Schools
The philosophy of Forest Schools is to encourage and inspire individuals of any age through positive outdoor experiences. Go to the website to find out about what happens at a Forest School, find one local to you, learn how to set one up and more.

www.forestschools.com

Index

First published in 2011
by Franklin Watts

Copyright © Franklin Watts 2011

Franklin Watts
338 Euston Road
London NW1 3BH

Franklin Watts Australia
Level 17/207 Kent Street
Sydney, NSW 2000

All rights reserved.

Series editor: Sarah Peutrill
Art director: Jonathan Hair
Designer: Jane Hawkins
Photography: Chris Fairclough,
unless otherwise stated

Dewey number: 643.1
ISBN: 978 1 4451 0221 4

Credits: Beata Becla/Shutterstock: 14tl.
Eleena Elisseeva/Shutterstock: 6tl.
Hibrida/Shutterstock: 2tl. Dave
Hughes/istockphoto: 11. Chung King/
Shutterstock: 4tl. Maragu/Shutterstock:
10tl. Romvo/Shutterstock: 12cr.
Scorpp/Shutterstock: 18tl. Smit/
Shutterstock: 12tl. Vaclav Volrab/
Shutterstock: 8tl, 9tr.
Every attempt has been made to clear
copyright. Should there be any
inadvertent omission please apply to the
publisher for rectification.

Franklin Watts is a division of Hachette
Children's Books, an Hachette UK
company. www.hachette.co.uk

The Author and Publisher would like
to thank Karen Constable, reception
class teacher at Mark First School in
Somerset, for her suggestions and help
with this series. Also thanks to the
school, especially the children, for their
enthusiasm, cooperation and sense of
fun during the photoshoots.

Printed in China

Important note: an adult should
supervise the activities in this
book, especially those near
water.